Pug's Hugs

Pug's Hugs
© 1999 Creative Teaching Press, Inc.
Written by Margaret Allen, Ph.D.
Illustrated by Keiko Motoyama
Project Director: Luella Connelly
Editor: Joel Kupperstein
Art Director: Tom Cochrane

Published in the United States of America by:
Creative Teaching Press, Inc.
P.O. Box 6017
Cypress, CA 90630-0017

CTP 2905

Pug the pup plays in the yard.
Pug digs and digs.

2

 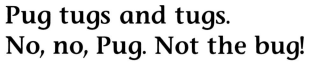

Pug tugs and tugs.
No, no, Pug. Not the bug!

3

Pug the pup plays in the van.
Pug pulls and pulls.

4

Pug tugs and tugs.
No, no, Pug. Not the cup!

Pug the pup plays in the den.
Pug grabs and grabs.

6

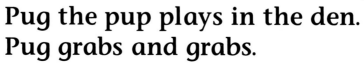

Pug tugs and tugs.
No, no, Pug. Not the rug!

But Pug tugs.
Pug tugs and tugs.

8

Here, Pug!
Come here!

9

Pug, stop!
Stop and sit.
Sit here.

Pug sits.

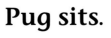

Then Pug jumps up.

Pug jumps and jumps.

Pug licks and licks.

Yes, yes, Pug.
Yes, lots of hugs!

BOOK 5: Pug's Hugs

Focus Skills: v, y, short u

Focus-Skill Words		Sight Words	Story Words
van	j**u**mps	come	den
yard	P**u**g	plays	licks
yes	p**u**p	then	pulls
b**u**g	r**u**g		
b**u**t	t**u**gs		
c**u**p	**u**p		
h**u**gs			

Focus-Skill Words contain a new skill or sound introduced in this book.

Sight Words are among the most common words encountered in the English language (appearing in this book for the first time in the series).

Story Words appear for the first time in this book and are included to add flavor and interest to the story. They may or may not be decodable.

Interactive Reading Idea

Have your young reader practice spelling words by writing -ug several times in a column on a piece of paper. Call out a consonant (p, h, d, r, b, j, or m) and have the child write it at the beginning of -ug. Ask your reader to spell the whole word letter by letter. Then, have your young reader blend the beginning sound onto the phonogram -ug and read the word.